WHEN A MAN FINDS A WIFE
He Discovers the Inside of God

⸂

Sherrie Norwood

© 2016 Sherrie Norwood

All rights reserved. No part of this publication may be reproduced or transmitted in any form or by any means, electronic or mechanical, including photocopying and recording, or by any information storage or retrieval system, without written permission from the author, excepting excerpts, which may be used for the purpose of review.

If you would like to share this book with another person, please purchase an additional copy for each recipient. Thank you for respecting the hard work of this author.

Scripture quotations marked ESV are taken from the Holy Bible, English Standard Version® (ESV®), copyright © 2001 by Crossway, a publishing ministry of Good News Publishers. Used by permission. All rights reserved. Scripture quotations marked KJV are taken from the Holy Bible, King James Version. Used by permission.

Word definitions taken from www.Merriam-Webster.com unless otherwise stated. Used by permission.

WHEN A MAN FINDS A WIFE
He Discovers the Inside of God

CONTENTS

ಐ

Introduction	i
1. Getting to Know HER	1
2. The Inside Out	9
3. THE Meeting	15
4. The Life – Getting to Know Her Produced Life	19
5. The Preface	23
6. The Lord is my Shepherd; I shall not want!	27
7. The Thirsty Man in the Beginning	29
8. The Thirsty Woman at the Well	33
9. Man, What Does Your Inside Say?	39
10. Getting to Know Her Again	45
11. Patience is a Virtue	49
12. A Clear Introduction	55
13. Ready to Embrace Her Time!	57
About the Author	78

Introduction

ಐ

This book was inspired by the moving of the Holy Spirit, and written by a woman that knows what it is like to function in the likeness of God. Not like God, not as God always, but in His likeness when it comes to the matters of her heart.

I struggled for many years with a pain that continuously piqued my curiosity concerning the love that God truly has for a woman. If she is to be loved as He loved the Church, then why isn't she being loved that way? Is it because man does not see her the way God sees the Church, or is it because the man has not been re-introduced to who she really is?

Or is it perhaps because she does not know who she is herself?

Regardless of what my questions were, I knew that many women out there were wondering: Has the "wo"man been forgotten, and how is she to be rediscovered again?

Whether she's trying to find the "wow" in herself or trying to get him to see the "wow" in her connection to him, she must know her value. She's priceless, and although it may seem that she's forgotten at times, it's okay to nudge him and remind him that she knows who she is.

While I was writing this book, I was in what would be considered a good place, although I had experienced some bad things. I was and still am determined to reach the hearts of men and women to remind them that we have a Kingdom assignment and that we must complete each task we are assigned.

As you read this book, keep in mind where we are as a body and how we were created to function as one. Also, be sure to remember the place in which the creation of man and woman took place. Visualize the spiritual and the natural operation that took place and is yet taking place today. Yes, we can get back to Eden and live on top of the world, because we're going to revisit the purpose and services ***"to-get-her"*** together again.

Your decision to read this book tells me that you're curious to know more about her (woman) and God. Not so that you become religious, but so that you learn how creative He is and understand how you were created to be in Him.

If you're a woman reading this book, you'll rediscover who you are; if you're a man, you'll see woman the way she was created to be seen in the beginning. Together, you'll discover the making of a beautiful new beginning.

1

Getting to Know HER

Ever wondered why she is the way she is, how she can forgive over and over to the point that she seems like a doormat or a glutton for punishment? She accepts and forgives and silently conceals her woes of sorrow when her strength is challenged or confronted. The term "wo" is a variant of the word woe, which simply means *a slight difference from, and in the form of, something else.* God created and fashioned the woman to be a slight difference from man. The woman was made from the rib of the man that is and was the inside of him. Man must realize where she came from: the very inside of the creation that was made in God's image and likeness. Getting to know her is the place in which the relationship is birthed, like the beginning God created.

Everything has a creation point, a beginning; and the true understanding of the development can be found in that beginning. She walks, talks, and acts slightly differently than he does and has a uniquely different fashion that makes her stand out in an expression of who she is. Have you ever considered that her fashion is from God? He formed the man, but He fashioned the woman. The Creator, our Creator, fashioned the design of the woman from the bone of the man—his rib (Genesis 2:23). She became a bone of his bone and flesh of his flesh. Therefore, it's no secret that she came from him, but the shame of the secret is that he sometimes fails to recognize that what was once inside of him now exists in her.

The woman is delicate and should be treated as such. Even God thought of her delicacy as something that would be pleasing, even in her beginning state. Her rare qualities were guarded from the very beginning and her delicacy required that she be handled with extreme care. God created the man and the animals from the dirt of the ground. He breathed the breath of life into the man, and the man became a living soul, which leaves the secret of life in the woman. This secret of how she became a living soul lies within the mystery of the Designer. The scripture does not reveal her first breath, yet she lived. The sleep that befell the man hovers over him yet again when he ignores the process of being awaked to her. Adam was excited about his gift from God, but not as excited as God was about His presentation to His creation. Until the man is truly awakened, he will not embrace the inside of God. More on this in the pages ahead.

It's strange how a man can become frustrated and agitated when she wants to communicate in her existence. His desire to become overwhelmed when she expresses herself can cause him to shut down and even run to another relationship when pressured, which is exactly how we treat God. Instead of running into His arms of protection, we tend to run away from Him until we realize we can't make it without Him, and that there is and should be no other.

The woman can provide nourishment and strength because she is the secret of he. He is to protect his secret, as she is to guard and not disregard his heart. Her position from the beginning was removed and placed in front of him, yet his portion remains without lack. He was still the man, but now with a greater connection to God's desire for him to be complete.

To know her takes an acknowledgment of her. No question of where she came from, how you don't get her, or may misunderstand her. Acknowledging her is recognizing that God has presented an extension of yourself to you. In His infinite wisdom, he put Adam to sleep so that the mystery of trust would forever be examined by those unafraid of being tested by her; and would forever be considered as the gift, the nurturer, the mystery of a life from a life, the inside of God.

Getting to know her is a process through which the man and the woman must be willing to trust God: understanding that they're not fully aware of why they're here, but more importantly, learning why they've been put together. The woman, having been fashioned after the man, is evidence that God has something for each of them to do.

But first, how is he the man going to get to know her without spending time with her? How is she ever going to trust him, since she has had to trust no man before?

Some relationships can start off with him showing her so much attention, the calling, the dating, and the reassuring that he's definitely into her. He takes the time to give her so much of himself that she's completely assured that he has awakened to the sense of who she is and what she needs. He's willing to try and give her the world.

This type of action from him should first begin with truth. The truth is he really has no clue of how to go about this without first getting his instructions from the Creator. He must be constantly before Him and asking, "What now?" and "Now what?" It's because the man has no clue as to what the woman needs or desires that so many relationships end up estranged. But who better to ask than the One that fashioned her and then gave her to him?

Why men aren't asking God what they need to do to love His fashioned one and why women aren't waiting for them to ask is a mystery to both genders. If we look back to the beginning of creation, we could try to come up with at least some rationale as to why. Therefore, I decided to ask God.

God, why is it that a man can see a woman, approach

her, and from that moment decide that she is the one?

When she accepts the acknowledgement and begins to trust him for who he says he is, what next?

Another interesting thought to ponder is, how much time is enough time for her to believe that he has her best interest at heart?

So, why approach in the first place? He can see her and have a strong desire to get to know her; but is he willing to take a deeper look? Can he truly handle the task of getting to know himself first before making the approach?

If a man is secure within himself to know that he won't play games with another human being's life, then that's a God sign that he's willing—willing to not lead her into places that he himself wouldn't be comfortable venturing. If they arrive at a place of uncertainty together, he's willing to seek God for further directions. After all, she's trusting him to lead.

Woman oftentimes can do what she was not designed to do, and that is to open up herself and allow a man to take from her what she was not fashioned to give. This is why the woman becomes so emotional and the man is so confused. He has no earthly idea how to deal with her emotions without seeking assistance from the One that created her. The man seeing her and wanting her is not enough to keep her happy or make her feel protected.

He sees what he wants and is bold enough to make the approach, but is he bold enough to spend time with the Designer to see how this thing works?

Now that he's confident that he sees what he wants, he has to cultivate the ground that he's pursing to cover. He has to nurture it and honestly have the desire to take care of it. The man should spend time with the woman and get to know what she needs in the seasons of life. Just like the earth that he was given from the beginning, he has to introduce her to his surroundings. The animals that he named should know her like they know him. They should know that she's nothing to be afraid of and that she has his best interest at heart. The man taking time with her helps her to trust that he's up for the task. Although the task may seem great, he can do it with the Help that gave her to him in the beginning.

As he spends time with her, she'll begin to feel protected and loved. She's confident in his ability to handle her because she can see how he's able to control the animals. The man has domain over the earth and God has domain over the man. She trusts the man because he trusts God, which makes her trust God as well. The man trains her thoughts to believe in the Creator because she sees how closely he trusts Him. Now he can see that she's willing to trust him because she believes in him just as she should.

When a Man Finds a Wife, He Discovers the Inside of God

He has to keep in mind that she's trusting his leading as he's being led by God. The process of getting to know her is a process that begins with him seeing the trust. He sees that she trusts him and he wants to do all that he can to maintain that trust. Not that she's not to trust God for herself, but that he's the first example of what trusting God looks like.

Can you imagine existing in a relationship and not understanding how the other being is able to believe in her existence? Eve knows where she comes from, but she has to trust Adam to understand where they're going daily because he knows the grounds. And not only does he know the grounds, he knows the ground rules. Having a clear understanding in the beginning of what the rules are if they're going to be pleasing to each other and to the Creator is extremely important.

QUICK RECAP
Getting to know her is knowing that she's the one that God created just for him. She's the one that God removed out of him and fashioned to fit in that place that feels empty without her. Getting to know her is acknowledging that if he's going to approach her, he should be prepared to love her as the woman that God has fashioned for him.

As he continues to get to know her, it's imperative that he continues to seek God for that which he may not understand concerning her. This is important because not knowing her inside could lead to needless and avoidable misunderstanding.

She knows who he is on the inside because this is where she comes from. She has the ability to feel things from him that she knows she can handle because she's connected to him in that place. The thing that she needs to know of him is existing outside.

2

The Inside Out

So, let the introduction begin from the inside out. The introduction may appear to be that of a strange encounter, but sometimes not looking on the inside could lead to a false reading of the packaged gift's contents. The misinterpretation can leave one disappointed and confused about what is actually expected.

In our relationship with God, we need to get to know more of Him from the inside out. In the same way, how much of you do we really need to know? Often when we come to God, we express our need for Him based on how we see Him, how we may articulate the introduction, and our need for Him. But at that beginning moment we really don't know Him, how He thinks, how He functions, or how He responds to our needs.

The pleasure of meeting someone does not stop at the first sight of him or her; it takes more encounters to detect the inner most parts and over time the real connection is made. Some may question whether there is such a thing as love at first sight and others may not even consider the thought, but let us look at what love is.

Love is the thing that catches you by surprise, the

unexpected of the expected and the desire to doubt. **God** is love, and when He presented the woman to the man, her appearance and *image* literally caught him by surprise. *This* marriage took place in the Garden of Eden and without reservation or hesitation Adam embraced her. Love again in action!

Adam embraced his gift simply because he knew that God had not only fulfilled a desire in his life, but also a need. When we delight ourselves in the Lord of our life, we're assured that our delight is exchanged for our desires. Doing good unto what God has blessed you with demonstrates an attitude to serve that which was given, and anything given without work is a gift. In other words, work is rewarded with pay and delight is rewarded with gifts.

When God sees a need, He responds with help. Since Adam was alone, his need was met by a helpmeet—God sent help to meet him. As God is a help to the man, he created Eve to be a help to the man as well. The term helpmeet always seems to be described as a helper to meet needs, but God's desire for man met man's desire for God.

"Inside out" expresses the impression to give of oneself in a way that's not selfish. When someone expresses himself or herself, the other is under the impression that what the person is saying will be evidence-based. The woman being the impression of the man's expression came through his desire

When a Man Finds a Wife, He Discovers the Inside of God

to have a mate. He was alone and looking for something that he could relate to, other than God and the animals.

Getting to see something that looks and feels like you can be a beautiful feeling. The man's inside is now outside and he now has the opportunity to see how he looks inside. He is now able to feel something that was produced out of him and manifested in her. The woman is an expansion of who he has been; the increase of his flesh has been manifested into her. The inside is now outside. From the beginning the man was the exterior and the woman was the interior. The outer and the inner, the inner and the outer. He and she together are one inside and out. The woman and the man were created to be one, so when a man finds a wife, they become one flesh. The inside of the man is the place that he can see and not be ashamed. The inside of the woman is the place that he can feel and not be ashamed to care. The two meeting the inside and outside of each other together is the place that makes the encounter an inside-out experience.

Some men may say that a woman just does not understand; however, she's willing to give the opportunity to know that she does. She's no stranger to getting into his feelings; but to him this is foreign because he had to be asleep while she was removed. When his eyes were finally opened, he saw her for the first time. Once she had that opportunity to see him awake, she was able to see that she was the extension of him. Her being outside of him and his being inside of her was yet another example of the inside-out meeting.

The two being one is what the woman being bone of his bone and flesh of his flesh means. They're now just that much into each other. She's now outside looking within and he is now inside looking within. The two are now considered as one because he now sees what his inside looks like on the outside and she knows where she comes from. Bone in and flesh out. His bone and his flesh in a fashion that is designed by God. Delicate to the touch and precious in her place of existence. She can do for him what the animals are unable to do and he is feeling the love.

Wonder what she's feeling when she sees him for the first time? Probably nothing, because when he saw her he was obviously in his feelings. He expressed his feelings for her in his reaction when she was presented to him. He was excited! She, on the other hand, was emotional. She was his spiritual part because she had been removed from his inner. She was his inner and psychological or spiritual side now manifested on the outside.

Ever thought about how often a man is always saying that women are so emotional? Well, ladies, don't take that statement lightly because "emotional" simply means that you are excited and open to displaying that excitement. So it's okay to be emotional, this isn't a curse. It's actually a blessing in disguise. However, he has to be open enough to accept this blessing that is open to give the inner affection and passion, and excited to demonstrate them emotionally.

Hearing many men and women say that women are emotional creatures is now music to my ears. I always had a strong desire to change or convert these feelings in some sort of way to please a man, but now I understand that this is exactly how I'm supposed to be. I'm an expression of what was removed from him and I'm excited to give that which he's missing. He may have a hard time getting in touch with that side of himself, but I'm here to give of myself that very thing.

The question is how does it feel to the man to meet his emotions? The feelings aren't mutual and the emotions aren't the same. Does he now not have emotions? Or does she not have feelings? Of course he feels for her, as God feels for her as well. She has emotions for him.

༃

With woman, the man now gained access to the inside of God through the interpretation of a woe—that thing that's a slight difference from, and in the form of, something else.

༄

3

THE Meeting

When Adam met Eve, it was like meeting the opposite side of the outside, which is the inside. Saying it this way may seem a little backward, but however we look at it, a mirror shows the reverse of what it sees. They were like the same person, but opposite. His chest was "in," hers was "out;" her genitals were "in," and his were "out." It's a little hard to see and say, but so is the act of looking in the mirror. The concept is the same when the woman and man meet. It can be difficult to see the images as the same but opposite, which is why every rib doesn't fit just any man's chest cavity.

This connection happens when the man meets his inside that makes him complete himself outside. She was a perfect fit while inside of him and should always fit his side outside and alongside him. She was brought out of him to adorn his side and to remain the protection of his inner parts. She has him covered because she knows what he really looks like on the inside. He has to trust her to do what she was fashioned to do, and that is to be his fashion. The question is, is he ready to meet her? The meeting has to take place.

The meeting was and is necessary to create an encounter that sums up the meaning of infinity; endless and beyond unlimited space. With woman, the man now gained access to the inside of God through the interpretation of a woe—that thing that's a slight difference from, and in the form of, something else. The wants and desires of the man literally touched the inside of God. Here's where the will of God brought on an action that confirmed that man only needs to be in line with His will to get what he desires. Adam moved the inside of God to gain favor with God when he was found in the will of God.

The man was in true fellowship with the Creator and using his Kingdom authority to name what he wanted and was to rule over. The animals and the earth were the man's domain, but he was still alone without a companion of his own. Until he was introduced to the inside of himself, he was incomplete; after all, he was created in God's image and His likeness, an extension of the Creator. Adam was rendered helpless and startled at the sight of her, and when he saw her, he saw himself.

When God made Adam, He had already made them when He took from the inside of Himself to fashion her. How amazing it is to know that she was with him at the beginning of His creation! She was with Adam all along, and the Father had to make sure he was ready to be opened for her. This state of a man's being is simple when we look at how he gets busy and forgets that he is alone. Now he will want her when the desire hits him. She's there when he's ready to be open and ready to give—ready to give of himself to her as her desire for him is ready to receive. He's the giver, and she's the receiver. She hears his heart loud and clear because she listens to his woes, desires, and yearning for her. As she appears before him, she's just like the feeling that he felt before she was formed. She is now in his feelings and hers, and there's no doubt that they belong together.

At this point, he's ready to know her. Before he gets to know her, though, **he has to be open**. God has to open him up to be prepared for her. This is how the inside is revealed. The man has to open up first if he's going to find a wife. Many women open up first as a sign of showing who she is, only to get hurt because she has not allowed him to open up first. What is he afraid of, and when does he allow her to open up to him when he knows that he should be opening up to her?

੶

What is Faith? It is the **F**ull **A**ssurance **i**n the **H**oly. The complete reassurance in the Saviour, the Giver, and the Sustainer who keeps on giving.

੶

4
❦

The Life – Getting to Know Her Produced Life

The external side of Adam was revealed when God had to take the inside of him to produce life. To begin the process, He pulled Himself out of Himself to cover and enclose that which could only be revealed once an awakening had taken place. The life producer was now at work. In His infinite wisdom, God could feel the man's desire churning as he worked the grounds, and his desires moved Him to do something for him.

It's interesting that Adam never asked God for the woman, but He knew that the need for her was there. The way a man lives should call for the movement of God to reveal the needs that he has. In other words, here was Adam doing what God had created him to do and without his having to say a word, God understood that he was feeling alone. The word of God declares that consequently faith comes by hearing and hearing comes from hearing the word (Romans 10:17). There had to be an unconscious belief from Adam that pulled on faith to act through God.

This type of hearing and acting was first demonstrated in the beginning when God created. When He spoke, Faith went to work and moved into creativity. Now that life had been created, life could use Faith, just like God. When God spoke to Faith and said that it wasn't good for man to be alone, it was as if Faith was responding again to "let there be." Remember in the beginning all God had to say was, "Let there be light" and there was light? Faith came by hearing God saying that it wasn't good for man to be alone, and faith had to move.

Do you get it?

Man's obedience to God moved Him to speak to the Faith, who heard and came to the creation party. Faith is obedient to God. Faith pleases God and without it, it's impossible to please Him. Faith produces things that we want, and it's the proof of the materials that we can't see. Sometimes we don't even know the materials we already possess because right now we can't see the production. Faith is now and now is Faith. Life was created by Faith and Faith came when it heard the voice of God. Faith comes when it hears.

What is Faith? It is the **F**ull **A**ssurance **i**n the **H**oly. The complete reassurance in the Saviour, the Giver, and the Sustainer who keeps on giving.

The man has to depend on God because He is the giver of life. The man has to depend on the woman because she is the carrier of life. The woman has to depend on the man because he is the trajectory of life, and when a man depends on God for everything, he lacks in no area of life. Man knows that in Him is life and life is supported by everything that He gives to man.

It's no different than when God gave the man the woman; she became life support to him. This support is all happening while she's still inside of him, and before she's brought out of him she has an assignment. While in him, she's attached to the assignment to support him. She's a delicate part of him, protecting those vital organs. His heart, lungs, and other vital parts are covered by her. She knows her place and she is secure where she is. He's complete with her, and she's connected to his completeness, his wholeness. She's now ready for her introduction to him because she knows who she is and where she is to come from, his inside. She understands his cave, so when he goes back inside, she knows just where he is.

This is a covenant relationship,
not a convenient relationship.

5
☙
The Preface

Now that creation was creating it was the thought of God that formulated the existence of the male and female in His image. From the moment He said, "Let us make man in our image and our likeness," the Trinity prefaced the book that we call the Bible, the living word of God. The prelude or forward to this book introduced the subjects, which were male and female, and expressed the purpose of their existence. This preface also acknowledged the assistance from the Son and Holy Spirit, which included the images of God.

The word of God states that He created male and female. He created them and said, "be fruitful and multiply and replenish and subdue." In other words, He said beautiful, multiply, replenish and subdue! He called her beautiful, him multiply, and commanded them to replenish and subdue! In order to make this command a reality, they had to get to know each other. This making was going to require some intimacy. Intimacy is to be close, familiar with; a togetherness that demands a friendship and a rapport. Getting to the level of "know" can be a tedious process if these elements are not present at all times. In other words, intimacy produces confidence in that which provides you warmth and affection.

It's no surprise when a sense of loneliness results from an intimate *act* that takes place before intima*cy*. Intimacy brings a sense of peace with its presence. This feeling may be hard to grasp because many think of intercourse, which is an intimate act, but not the total inclusion.

Let's look at intimacy. "In-" is used as a functioning word describing the location and a position within limits. "In" describes a position that sets one up for promotion. Have you ever heard someone say "I just need to get in," "get my foot in the door," or "I'm in there." Well, that's exactly what intimacy does. It gets you in. It may start with the foot in the door; that's how all entries are made, and then guess what? You're in there.

We have to be passionate about our walk together with Christ as well as with each other. Intimacy creates that bond, so we have to be careful with whom we choose to be intimate. When a man finds a wife, he should seek to inti-mate her, not intimidate her or be intimidated by her. What this means for the relationship is that the mates must date. This is frequent contact, getting to know her from the inside out. As he discovers her, he discovers himself. Now don't get me wrong, this process can be intimidating; however, it's a process that he must be willing to encounter if he is going to get in.

The Bible speaks a little about the relating between the man and the woman in the book of Genesis, which tells us that there may be only a little relating in any marriage relationship. When we think of how men relate to women, it's like the north and the south, the east and the west all traveling in different directions but in a cross relationship.

Did I say cross relationship? Does that mean a covenant relationship?

Yes, it does.

This is a covenant relationship, not a convenient relationship.

It can seem confusing when you don't know the signs in the relationship or directions of the relationship. This is when time spent with the Maker or Creator of the compass has to be the source of the relationship. A soldier in the military may find that one of the hardest parts of training is the understanding of land navigation. One can be lost without a guide or leader, but he won't get lost if he knows where he's going with a compass.

☙

If God so loves the world that He gave His only begotten, which was and is His absolute best, then what do you consider to be better than Him?

❧

6
ಐ

The Lord is my Shepherd; I shall not want!

Because He is your shepherd, He knows what you want. He's the guide to your needs; the Shepherd is the compass to your meet. But you must realize that you can't get to the Father without going through the Son. You must come past or through the Son to get to the Father, and what good is it if you have the instrument, but refuse or decide not to use it? You are lost without a cause because you have the tool to reach where you are trying to go; however you have failed to use it for its worth.

Just like our Creator is here and ready to guide us.

What sense does it really make to not utilize the source or resource? God as our resource is the gift that keeps on giving. One can draw from Him in order to function effectively.

Now, you may be wondering, what does this have to do with the subject matter of the woman, the wife, the gift? If God so loves the world that He gave His only begotten, which was and is His absolute best, then what do you consider to be better than Him? Here's the connection: The Father and the Son are one; so the Father knows how to give His best to his children. We know that He so loved the world that He gave his best, His only, so that all who would believe would have non-perishing life. Well, that's just who He is, and if we believe in Him, we receive of Him.

The Shepherd knows the needs of His sheep. God was Adam's Shepherd, and He made sure that man didn't want. Adam wanted a helpmeet and God, being his Father, helped him to meet his help. The strange thing about a shepherd is that he needs the sheep to trust him, and a sheep is so trusting that it's willing to be led. Adam had to trust that when the Father gives, He gives the need the "meet" that it needs to survive. I know that we are not talking about natural meat, but in this case the meat that was needed for the man to survive the loneliness was the meet, the mate. So He gave the woman as the meeting of his need and He gave to the need it met. In other words, He met the need of a thirsty man.

7

The Thirsty Man in the Beginning

He sees it, he wants it, and has to have it. Well, what is it that he really wants? He goes out looking in all the wrong places, but what exactly is he looking for? Is he looking for love, or is he lusting for love? Has he forgotten where love is, and why isn't love responding to him? For God so loved the world that He gave; He gave because mankind was in need of a savior. Man had forgotten his first love, so he was missing the presence of love.

Now that he's lost and needing to survive the separation, he needs something that's going to satisfy his thirst.

After seeing everything that he had named existing and coexisting in their elements, he is thirsty, and God knows it. The man is in a constant rotation when he's not complete. He's searching for his rib, and she's out there somewhere crying out for him to find her. She may be in a place that she knows she does not belong, but she is yet waiting to be found. How did she get there, and where was he when she was introduced the first time? Did he get busy and fail to respond to the call? She's calling, but somebody failed to respond, so what does she do? She eats from the forbidden and causes him to partake in the separation too.

Many young men and women know about this experience. They can feel a connection from the beginning and just as she is ready to respond to his "wow," he's "know"-where to be found. He seemed so interested in the beginning and now that she is ready for his attention he is not answering or calling anymore. Yes, he is know-where to be found—that knowledge of her is lacking. Men perish for the lack of know-ledge (Hosea 4:6).

You knew her first, so what if she drifted? It was and still is your responsibility to go to God for her and after her. She is going to get into something that she never should have from the beginning, because God gave you the instructions. This is why the restoration has to take place because many women have gone to too many forbidden places and eaten. He is out of line because he had no business partaking in that separation and she had no business straying.

Now what?

It's not too late to restore that broken place because the contract is yet intact. Man, getting back to your first love is what it is really all about. This is in no way suggesting that every woman you thought was your first love is where you should be. I am simply saying that you are sometimes given the opportunity to get back to that place of knowing who your first love is, the one that completes you and you know

When a Man Finds a Wife, He Discovers the Inside of God

that you are incomplete without. You may have made some mistakes in that place but know now what you have, and you are going to love her like the first time. You are willing to hold her like the first, and it will always be a first time every time.

It's so important to remember the Creator when you are young, because you have a lot more years to enjoy the pleasures of her. Not to say that the later years are any less fulfilling, because good wine becomes greater later. The thirsty man does want his thirst to be quenched, and if he lets patience have her way he won't want any other stream. Believe you me, she has been thinking about you and longing for you for a very long time. She may have been in the uttermost, gutter most parts of life, yet she still feels you. She knows that what she feels is real because she can't stop thinking about you. She knows what you need, and God knows how to give that thing you need to you. She desires to quench your thirst and hers for you. Not just in the flesh, but in the natural and the spiritual.

She's what the Father calls the good thing. She is the God thing and that good thing.

☙

God asked Adam basically the same question that He asked the woman at the well: "Adam, where is your mate?"

❧

8

The Thirsty Woman at the Well

The word declares in the fourth chapter of John that when Jesus met the woman at the well, she was drawing water to quench a thirst. The woman's encounter with Jesus was on a natural level, but the Spirit is always present in the natural to meet the spiritual and the natural need if the person is open to receive. Jesus says to the woman, "Everyone who drinks of this water will be thirsty again, but whoever drinks of the water that I will give him will never be thirsty again" (John 4:14, ESV). The funny thing about this passage is, in today's time, the younger generation refers to a woman that desires many men as being "thirsty." You see, there is nothing new under the sun. This woman was "thirsty." Oh yes, she was thirsty for something that the men she had could not satisfy, so Jesus had to kill that thirst altogether. Therefore, He gave her satisfaction when He opened up and revealed himself to her.

(We may be on to something...keep reading.)

Jesus had to get the woman to trust (to thirst for) Him by telling her to go and get her husband. She had a man, but he was not her own husband. In other words, "name him, the one you got, he is not yours." The story goes on to say that Jesus revealed to her that He already knew the truth about her: she had been married five times, and the one that she was with was not hers. She was there at the well alone, looking for something to quench her thirst, and apparently it had not been revealed in anything that she had already seen. It was at this moment that Jesus opened Himself up to her and began to reveal Himself from the inside. He told the woman, "God is Spirit, and those that worship Him must worship Him in spirit and truth." The woman replied, "I know the Messiah is coming (he who is called Christ). When he comes, he will tell us all things." Jesus said to her, "I who speak to you am he" (John 4:16-26, ESV).

So now let's go back to the beginning in the garden when Adam had to be put to sleep because he was thirsty, just like this woman. Adam had a conversation and encounter with God, just as this woman did with Jesus at the well. Well, well, well, when did this meeting take place? In the second chapter of Genesis, Adam is naming all of the animals that the Lord God is forming from the ground. God brought these animals to Adam to see what he would call them, and according to what Adam called them, they were so named. So Adam had an unspoken desire that God knew of as he met Adam with the animals.

Stay with me as we go back and forth from the woman at the well to the man in the field.

Every beast of the field, every fowl of the air, every living creature now had mates, but Adam had yet to meet his. So God said, "It is not good that man should be alone; I will make him a help meet for him" (Genesis 2:18, ESV). If you look at the scripture carefully, **before he formed the beast and the fowl out of the ground, He made the above statement concerning the loneliness of the man.** This break in creation may be a little hard to grasp because many of us have been taught by hearing rather than by reading some things for ourselves.

(So now you know you'll need to go back and read Genesis 2.)

Moving on, let's look at this marvelous spiritual and natural encounter. God knew the spiritual need of Adam before the natural meeting took place. So God gave the man instructions for living in the Garden and the trees that he could eat from and the one that he should not eat of; then He said to Himself, "It is not good that man should be alone" (Genesis 2:18, ESV). Now, God asked Adam basically the same question that He asked the woman at the well: "Adam, where is your mate?" As Adam was naming the animals, God is saying neither of these belongs to you. Adam named all of the cattle and the fowl, but the Bible said there was not found a help meet for him (Genesis 2:20). It's then that God caused a deep sleep to fall upon Adam. And while Adam slept, He took one rib of the ribs that He could've chosen from and closed up Adam's flesh, instead of taking two or leaving Adam awake while He fashioned the one. Yes, He fashions the one!

HE FASHIONS THE ONE

Yes, He fashions the one for you, Brother Adam. She doesn't look like the beast of the field or the fowl of the air. With a bust, she looks like you.

So when Adam saw her, he saw himself, just like when God created Adam, He saw Himself. One created in His image and His likeness. Adam now saw someone created in his image and in his likeness; she was just the opposite of who he saw, yet was. He saw what God had fashioned from what was inside of him. He saw what was supposed to represent the inside of God; after all, only God knows what he looks like on the inside and He created man and woman in His image inside and out.

But what about His likeness? What was God like on the inside? When He completed His image of Adam, He didn't reveal His likeness to him. The way He revealed His likeness was by putting His image to sleep to open up Himself to fashion His likeness onto that rib. The one rib removed from Adam was now fashioned in God's likeness to be a bone of his bone and flesh of his flesh. Just as God didn't allow Adam to see the inside of his own self, he didn't allow Adam to see the inside of Himself.

When a Man Finds a Wife, He Discovers the Inside of God

Many men go through and have gone through life looking for the one. The one that they can relate to, the one that they can name and call their own. The one that they can give their last name. Adam was no different. God allowed Adam to add Glory to his name. Man was the last name and "Wo" was the first name of the beginning of Woman. The Glory of God is simply in the "Wo." The woman is one of the many signs and wonders of who He is. God never stops "wo"-ing" us or wowing us. He's a <u>wo</u>nder in our souls and He is <u>wo</u>nderful. Now the man that also shares that image and likeness of God can add Glory to his name when he marries her and gives of his glory, which shall be his last name.

I Corinthians 11 speaks of Christ being the head of every man, and the head of the woman is man. 1 Corinthians 11:7 lets us know that the man is the image and glory of God; but the woman is the glory of man. Let's not lose focus—this isn't up for argument or debate, because the scripture also lets all know that in the Lord woman is not independent of man, *nor is man independent of woman.* For as woman came from man, so also man is born of woman, but everything comes from God."

৩

When a man finds a wife, he rediscovers what the Father is like.

৩

9

Man, What Does Your Inside Say?

When she says something to you, do you believe her for what she says? What does your inside say? This discussion is to be had when a man finds a wife, not a struggle. When you have a discussion, is she saying something that makes you uncomfortable inside? Do you listen to your inside?

Well, when she says something, it is okay to listen to your inside. If you can evaluate what your gut is saying, then you can do the same with her. Sometimes we treat God the same way—as if we don't need Him. We are guilty of not following His leading from the inside out. Internally, we are fighting with the One that has our back, our side, and our front.

The woman is to protect the inside of man, just as the man is to protect the outside and inside of the woman. He is responsible for making sure she looks the way they both feel. Now, this is not to say that he is going to feel well all the time, this is only in the natural sense. In the spiritual, when the awakening takes place, he should always do his best to present himself with care to the Creator. He is to remember the Creator and the creation party as if it only took place a few minutes or seconds ago. The problem with man is that for so long he has been going through life without the reflections that would keep him grounded. The very depth of his existence is not to be forgotten, which is why she is constantly reminding him to look at her and not forget why she was made: just for him.

When you see him, you see her, and when you see them, you see God. His image and His likeness.

This bud is for you.

This beautiful creature begins as a part of something great. The ribs of the man, broken off into one. The rib is delicate yet strong in its existence. It knows its place and what it was fashioned to do. She, being an intricate part of man, cannot bear not to be covered or not cover him in those vital areas. The man's flesh was opened up; a bone was removed and re-covered, "recovered."

Just like our Father and His Son.

Jesus was in the beginning, He was broken off from His Father, yet they remain as one. He was removed from His Father to cover and recover that which was created. The mission was for restoration and getting back to Eden where creation took place. The man is to get back to creation by restoring Eden. Many homes, families, and lives are broken because the man has left Eden and ruined the operation. With frustration and disgust, he finds himself empty and longing for something that he is sleeping on. He cannot get back to the place of restoration because he himself is not in fellowship.

Although we have been looking at the woman and her likeness to the man, what about the man's likeness to God? According to Merriam-Webster.com, the word likeness simply means to be similar to, to have a resemblance, but also implies a closer correspondence than similarity, which often implies that things are merely somewhat alike. Why would we have a closer correspondence than similarity? Because when we open up to one another, we have closer communication than a resemblance. We may not look the same, but we can have closer communication when we open up and give up something of ourselves. God in His infinite wisdom gave Adam something and shared something with Adam that He Himself had also experienced in a relationship. When Adam was created, he walked and talked with God. He met his Creator in the cool of the day after a long hard day, and they communicated. Nowadays that relationship hardly exists because man is too tired to open up. The world system has been adopted and, therefore, we lack communication. For God so loved the world that He presented His only begotten Son.

And God so loved His creation that He presented a woman to him, someone that he could talk to and relate to.

When a man finds a wife, he rediscovers what the Father is like. This may seem like a hard pill for some men to swallow;

however so is this world system. Man has gotten so far away from the Kingdom that he forgets to seek it first. Instead, he tries everything else before he goes back to the Creator who provided what he needed even without him having to ask. The Church is full of women, seeking the face of God, when the man was the first to seek and encounter God's face and presence. He worked and talked with God, seeking to please Him. Where has this commitment gone? Why isn't one enough? Why does he seek for more when God has given him one? Granted, there are many relationships that a man has thought to be the one and the woman as well, simply because he sees something that his flesh desires and he goes after it. But know he has a chance to rediscover since his eyes have been reopened. Yes, I said *know* he has a chance and not "now" because now he needs to know that he has been given another chance to know her. That's called the know-ledge.

Although separated from the beginning, the connection yet remains. Just as our Heavenly Father and His presentation were separated in the beginning, Jesus remained as a part of the Kingdom. Some people have said that there's old school and new school; however the old is still connected to the new. As a part of the old man that was put to sleep, the woman still has that connection and that longing to be connected. Why do you think she's always asking for your time? Because she wants to be connected. Why do you think she's always asking for you to communicate? Because she wants to be connected. She'll always want to be connected because she's a part of who you are. Now that she's apart from you, she wants to continue to remind you that she's a part of you.

☙

As you spend that time loving her like Christ loves the Church, you'll give your life for her, just like He did. The great thing about love and giving your life for it is that you only have to die to self because Jesus already died for us all.

☙

10

Getting to Know Her Again

We all know that the scriptures give reference to Adam knowing his wife. The intimate part of knowing her was the physical attraction. Now, what are you going to do after you know her, my friend and brother? You should continue to get to know her, and know her well.

Why do I say know her well? Well, because that's exactly what the depth of the relationship will be all about. Knowing her well. Knowing her deeper than you have before, taking the time to experience her in her depth. Just as Jesus said, "Whoever has seen me has seen the Father" (John 14:9, ESV); as you've seen her, you should see yourself. Why is this so different now than the first time that you took a look? It's because you're going to have to know her again.

Men have gotten away from realizing the precious price that was paid for this relationship, just like we sometimes forget the price that was paid for us to have that relationship with God. We're missing the creation because our eyes have lost focus of what true relation is all about. The Bible instructs man through Jesus to love the Lord with all of his heart, soul, and mind. Other passages add strength to that list. In other words, however you look at the love, it's deep. Getting to know her requires learning the depth of loving her. Loving her is knowing her and knowing her is loving her. The man is to love his wife as Christ loved the Church and gave Himself up for her.

Who is "her"? In Ephesians 5:25, she is the Church. God loved the Church, "man," so much that He gave himself up for her. We know that according to the Bible God loved us so much that He gave. Yes, He gave himself up for the world. Man, I know it's hard, but you have to love to give and give to show your love. Remember, this is how you are commanded to love her. How many times have you heard a woman say to a man, "show me that you love me"? Probably more times than you care to think about that particular task. So from now on, instead of looking at it as a task, remember that it's a command. As you spend that time loving her like Christ loves the Church, you'll give your life for her, just like He did. The great thing about love and giving your life for it is that you only have to die to self because Jesus already died for us all.

It's time for man to get back to the restoration of creation or we'll continue to see marriages and families decline. Brothers and sisters, we're a long way from home and the Kingdom continues to suffer this violence. This violation has to be corrected, and the fine has to be paid in order to get back to right standing or the right position. Righteousness is a quality of being morally right or justifiable. Man's righteousness is justifiable when it is pleasing to God. A man finding a wife is a good thing and pleasing to God. It's justifiable to please her as Christ is pleasing to the Church. Loving her is what He died for, and in dying for her He showed his love for her.

When God put Adam to sleep, he literally died for her. Remember, this isn't a physical death, but self-death. Can you imagine how this world would be changed if men were to get back to righteousness or right standing? To a man, this means that he needs to lay down and let the surgery begin on the inside and be fashioned on the outside.

ೞ

The missing piece of it all in some relationships is the patience and the virtue--the endurance and the quality to endure, respectively. The ability to wait and the position of righteousness while waiting.

ಙ

11

Patience is a Virtue

The way to get to know her is through patience. Yes, time. Over time, you will learn that this is a slow process. Taking time to do it is a virtue; it's a behavior and a Kingdom principle. The Bible talks about patience and calls patience "her." James 1:4 (KJV) says, "But let patience have her perfect work, that ye may be perfect and entire, wanting nothing." In other words, in a relationship it's important to be patient with her, like God is patient with you. If you let patience work, it will work. This place isn't an easy place, especially when it comes to a man dealing with a woman.

What is patience? It's being able to accept or tolerate and handle problems without being annoyed. Patient(s) are also those in need of attention. So who can find a virtuous woman? A man that's patient and willing to give her attention. One who possesses the ability to tend to her and her needs. Who has the ability to treat her virtue with respect.

If you look in depth at what patience and virtue are, you'll see that patience is he and virtue is she. The reason that many relationships fail is that he doesn't recognize her and she can't feel him. The missing piece of it all in some relationships is the patience and the virtue. The endurance and the quality to endure, respectively. The ability to wait and the position of righteousness while waiting. In many cases, this is done all wrong. They mate before dating. Dating should always be a part of the mate, or they'll mate before they wait. If you wait to get what you need, you won't want for anything because she'll be all that you need. She'll be perfect for you because she'll meet your desires and you'll meet her needs. The relationship will only lack one thing outside of the two and that is the individual relationship with God. Together you can become one in Him.

Man, this may seem so far away from home. How in the world do we return?

We must get back to Eden, the garden, the plain land. Let's get back home, to the garden that was well kept. Where the man appreciated the pleasure of the land. The plain view, the land view.

I was intrigued when I looked up the meaning of plains. Wikipedia defines it this way: "In a valley, a plain is enclosed on two sides but in other cases, a plain may be delineated by a complete or partial ring of hills, by mountains, or cliffs."

Highs and lows, lows and highs. For the man, this can be a scene of emotions; for the woman, this can be a place of protection. The garden has many views, some more plain than others. Getting through it all is a process before getting to see all and knowing all of it. This sometimes-difficult process is evident if a man has ever had to deal with a woman (not a "real" woman, because she is real. Some are just more complete or partial than others; however they are still real women: real emotions, highs, lows, hills, mountains, cliffs, and all).

She may have times when she appears to be complete, then there are times when she lacks the confidence within herself. Now he has the opportunity to reassure her that he's there to protect who she is and where she is. After all, she gets it from him. She gets where she is from him. It's safe for her to be plain with him; she knows it's all a part of the process of Eden restoration. As with the Father, there's a process before we see Him in all of His glory. The man that sees his wife in her plain state knows the beauty that she yet possesses. She owns it, and she knows it. She has to be confident that he knows where she came from and that he understands the pain in that place. She's his rib, his bone, and there's a space of flesh that separates his chest from hers. The desire to connect should always remain in their existence for one another. There will be times of loneliness and longing; however there is a forever unspoken bond between the two, always acknowledging each other and the connection. When you see me, you see him, when you see him, you see me. It's oh so beautiful.

Man, you're looking for her, you've got her. Man, you have her, you've got her. He that asks shall receive, he that seeks shall find, and He that knocks, the door shall be open (Matthew 7:7). This task is the dilemma that some men are in right now. If you are in a relationship, this is an opportunity for you to decide if you have found your wife. Have you come to realize that you may have been sleeping on the presentation that has been brought to your attention? Are you ready to open up and embrace your gift? After all, she's your inside. Truly this is a matter of whether she is a good woman and if she is good for you and to you. If not a temporary fix, you have the authority to subdue and have dominion over her, which means you have the right to pacify and protect her. I know you were probably looking for that strong arm to have power over her, but your role is to love and protect her. The initial questions that come to mind when one is thinking about finding a wife may lead to endless questions, but you have the power to name her.

And how do I speak to the man that is doing his best to right his wrongs? I say to you, my brother, there's no better time to begin than right now. Now faith will produce the power to restore you back to your right state. Not all relationships that begin will last, and the ones that last after the ones that ended will become new, simply because God makes all things new. God has the ability to restore the years that the cankerworm and the locust have eaten up (Joel 2:25). He can restore that which may seem like a loss as you express that desire to allow restoration to take place.

I know you want peace, and peace you shall have. You shall have love, peace, patience, and joy. Yes, she shall fulfill your desire for these places of intimacy. You can expect for her to give you good pleasures when you are loving her like Christ loves the Church. It's not too late to begin again. It's not too late to start over. When you find her, love her and protect her. Remember who she is as you give of yourself to her. Have patience for her and be patient with her when you have her.

It's my prayer that some man is reading this book and finding the strength to open his eyes to what he has in front of him. I pray that you will begin to allow God to speak to your heart, as the protector of it is yet attached to it.

For the man that has a wife, for the man that is seeking a wife, for the woman that has been found, and for the woman that's waiting to be discovered, this book is for you. The moment that the introduction takes place it must be a Kingdom connection—the kind that no matter how much effort you have put into it before, you are ready to make a new connection.

Sherrie Norwood

    I know there will be some men that may say, "I love my wife and I am loving her like a man is supposed to love a woman." But have you truly discovered the gifts that are within her, and have you discovered the extended version of yourself? A man that has a wife and knows how to love and protect her is sincerely concerned about her and the things that concern her. He is willing to forsake all others just for her. This man has discovered that she is the one thing that keeps him grounded and has the loving ability to make him feel as though he is above everything. He knows how to please her and is eager to do so. He cannot imagine life without her and is thankful for the gift that keeps on giving. A man that has found a wife knows that it takes a lot of patience to handle the pressure of keeping what God has blessed him with. He knows that he has to continue to till and nurture the grounds that he was ordered to keep. The vows in the ceremony were for you to love her, comfort her, honor and keep her.

12

A Clear Introduction

Let me make her introduction clear: She is all that. She is "Her," who she is, her past, her present, and her future. She had to be her to get here. And she had to be there to get "her" status. She is about to rediscover who she is by accepting everything that she has gone through to get to where she is now. It doesn't matter where she is; her breakthrough is coming through.

Yes, she's finally breaking-through and being through with being confused, through with settling for less than best, and through with taking the backseat because she knows that she belongs out front. It's where God placed her in the beginning—for her to be seen on the scene.

I know some have heard that in order for her to be found she must be hidden, but some of us have been hiding for too long, ashamed to come out to the world because of our past location. But every "good thing" has to come forth, whether dead or alive. From the right command, it must come forth. To be found she must be seen, in her best-fashioned design, which is herself. Not putting on make-up to hide her scars, but embracing every scar that led her to her healing and revealing.

Sherrie Norwood

Why stay in the dirt, the clay, the mud, when God brought her out of that, when He fashioned her with a grace that got man's attention in the beginning? She won't worry about who doesn't want her anymore, but she will be revealed and available for the one who needs her, the one that's ready for her, and ready to make her a part of the assignment that he was given. Yes, you see, when you see him you see her, and when you see her you see him, and together you see them as one.

Don't worry, she doesn't mind waiting for her time of revelation, for this will be her time to be unveiled and presented. She'll be just right for the introduction. No longer will she be afraid to be shown off by the one that she was fashioned for. Her beauty, smarts, elegance, and grace will show him no mercy. He will know that he has a packaged deal. Just like that beautiful bride behind the veil. Her time from Genesis to Revelation (reveal-action) is right here and right now. Her breakthrough is about to break through the pain, the hurt, the fear, and the break. Oh yeah, even the Break! From that point where she felt like she was not worthy of life, life is about to come forth. She's about to live in the life in which she was fashioned and designed to live. Her, here, he, and he, here, her. She is ready to be complete in he and he is ready to be whole again with her. They are together and to-get-her makes them one. A bone of his bones and flesh of his flesh.

13

Ready to Embrace Her Time!

Her time is here whether she is ready or not; she must come out. And although detached from the body, she is still attached to the assignment, and she must be ready to be led for the purpose of the commission—the together mission, which is the coexisting assignment. And like God, the man now will experience the separation but understand the forever connection. She had to exit to exist. She is now existing, but as the Father and the Son are one in existence, so are they, male and female, established on the earth. She has been separated from him, but is forever connected to him.

God in His infinite wisdom knows how to divide one but keep them whole together as two. It is never too much for God to get through to divide him to get two complete ones. God is able to reach you, and He can bring you out of something without a struggle. After all, He's the Master of the whole operation. He's in the completing business, and He wants us to complete one another, not compete with one another. The male has his assignment, and the female has hers. The assignments are not shaped the same, but they function the same way.

Both will be used for the Glory of God. Her assignment may appear to be a little bigger to her than his at times, but he will cover and protect her at all times. They were designed this way.

She knows how much protection she is for him because of where she comes from; it's an inside job. So when a man finds a wife, she doesn't have to be hidden, she just has to be discovered from his inside. She has to touch him in that empty place. He knows what he is missing and what he needs to make him complete again. And she is willing to embrace the task. **It's not a fight, it's a fit.**

She doesn't have to fight to get in, they're a perfect match. She doesn't desire to be there just because he's feeling her, but she is clear about where she belongs. She's not to be deceived by all of the cavities (chests) that approach her— the too-sweets that just need a filling or the already rotten that are just trying to get the pull. You see, the relationship begins with him feeling her and her filling him again.

IT'S "HER" TIME EMBRACE HER
It is her time and her time is now. She's ready to begin the work that she is cut out specifically to do. Man can't do what she does, and she wasn't designed to do his work. Her work is what she was cut out for. The drastic cut doesn't mean that

she has lost anything, yet she has gained her independence. She can depend on him for moral support, but she has to do her part to get her reward. Getting to know who she is takes some alone time, some to reflect on where she came from and what her purpose is for being her on this earth. She must come to a place of understanding separation in order to appreciate the one that will make her life complete in impartation.

Yes that part: the part that she is to play in carrying the life that will give life. She must learn to cope with some of the removals in life, because some things had to be cut for other things to live. She must carry the assignment to reproduce with her mate yet carry alone, which is not a punishment but a testament of her assignment. Now that she is here, she must embrace her time. Woman, embrace you; Man, embrace her and let God embrace you together as one.

ALLOWING GOD TO OPERATE

Allowing God to operate takes a time of preparation, processing, and recovering. We must be prepared to trust him through the process and understand that every emotion attached to the pain is real, but simply a part of the process. The problem is we don't always wait for our complete healing because we're eager to get back to our old selves. But if we truly think about it, the reason for a surgery is to fix a problem and to make us better. The Master Surgeon knows exactly what we need; we only need to allow Him to master His piece of creation. We don't always get full restoration when we rush the healing process.

What athlete that's serious about playing sports would have surgery and leave the hospital the same day to play in the Super Bowl or the NBA finals? Right. He's not ready.

When we ask God to fix something in our lives, we have to allow Him to work. As we trust in His ability to fix our ask, all we have to do is wrap our faith around the healing daily, not anxiously, but patiently waiting for His strength to be made perfect during our weakness. Wrapping our faith around our healing takes an exercising of execution. Yes, we must exercise our faith while waiting on that perfect strength to move effectively again. Just because we don't feel like moving, doesn't mean that healing isn't happening. We want everything that we want *right now*. Unfortunately, life doesn't always work that way. Some broken things take a little longer to heal than others. Healing is fundamental, and we must get up and move when we're able daily to prevent stiffness from setting: to set us back, set us still, or set us up for failure. It is called faith in motion, faith in action, and faith in God.

SHE BLEEDS AS A WAY OF LIFE

She bleeds as a way of life to position her body to give life. She doesn't bleed for life, just as a part of life and for the reproduction of it.

Woman, you may feel like a fraud sometimes, giving and encouraging and not believing in your own worth; but wo-man let me stop you. You are authentic, the absolute real thing. Many salute you, but sometimes you forget to salute yourself for coming, for going, and for giving. Now it's your time to receive for life. It's your time to live and breathe the beauty that was already set before you hit the scene. You need a coming out party and not a pity party. You need a celebration just because you have a reason to celebrate. The flows and issues of life that you may encounter are only to make you ready for life.

Just because she has gone through some challenges, issues, and times of purification, doesn't mean that life isn't coming. Some things are just going to stop for her to carry the blessing to its full birthing term.

Ladies and gentlemen, the pain is what it is and it can be described as *the point of and an instant notice that something is wrong*. When the man sees her, his pain of loneliness begins to reduce itself to a mere "not alone anymore." He may seem to act alone but he knows that she is there to give him what the beast can't, what the wild ones will not, and what the fowl refuses. His many encounters with the animals can make him feel as if that is where he belongs. **However, he needs to recognize that they, the animals, are not of his kind and unless he separates himself, he will be as they are.** God blessed the woman and the man and commanded them to subdue the earth, not to subject themselves to the lifestyle of the animals. They were now given the freedom to reproduce themselves; in other words, increase themselves in number to fill the earth and to continue to fulfil the duties and responsibility of mankind. Although the woman was fashioned after the man was created, she was blessed when he was blessed and together they were commanded to rule.

Many women are questioning their existence and wondering why on earth they're continuing to run into the same issues as it relates to a man. Well, dear woman, I believe I was created and inspired to help you out with this question. The reason why women are questioning and the man is not answering is that he apparently doesn't truly know who you are, which begs a question: If he doesn't know who you are, then does he perhaps not know who God is?

After many years of struggling with the question "what's wrong with me?" I have finally gotten to the bottom of my questions and guess what answer I found? Nothing. **There is absolutely nothing wrong with you.** All you are required to do in the waiting process is to wait for his eyes to be opened. I have communicated with the young and the old and each time I hear "what did I do wrong?" or "what's wrong with me?" I am happy to answer their question. If you are a good thing, then there is no-thing wrong with you. So wait on that man to be awakened by God.

Take the woman in the Bible with the issue of blood. There were probably many times that she allowed her issue to stop her from flowing in calling. In other words, she was more comfortable flowing in her issue because it had become her way of life. Now that she had spent all of self-gain and energy, she had nothing else to spend. She did not even have the time to spend as she had in the past because the flow had robbed her of years wasted on things that did not resolve the issue. So what is she to do now? Well, ladies, one sure thing is that woman was fashioned with a tenacity that allows her to tap into a strength that will drive her into overtime. When she feels like she can't go on, there is a point of contact that pushes her past the pain and to the promise. When she has reached that level of maturity that she knows is unlike the past, but she can recognize the past trying to creep into her promise, she's going to do something about it. What is it that she is going to stop? The first thing she needs to do is stop blaming herself for the issue. She has to realize that just because she's a woman this issue is going to exist; however, it doesn't have to control her life. She has to come to the point in which she's in control of her life and the issue is just a part of her life that she has to live with until her time of deliverance.

HIS REACTION TO SEEING HER

The introduction of the woman to the man was about his reaction to seeing her for the first time, not her reaction to seeing him. The introduction of her was more about her actions and his reaction. She was now here, existing, and he was excited about her presence. She was his precious gift from God. The Master of Creation had done it again for him, giving man something of Himself. This time it was an extension of man and an intention of God. The intention was to cause the extension of Adam to exist. What was once inside of him would now live outside of him. She would forever from this point coexist with him to add something to his being. Being all that he needs by his side. She would love and cover him, protecting his heart that was in the right place for her from the beginning.

What did he see when he saw her? What was she thinking of

him before he actually woke up? She had her act together before his eyes were opened. A good woman has the ability to stay in place, a high place so that she can hear. Sometimes being so low will cause you to not be able to hear as clearly. Rising above the noise is a sign of maturity; when you can elevate your thoughts to a point of alleviation, you will begin to see the growth.

TRUE LOVE
He that finds a wife discovers true and unconditional love. She will love him even in his messiest state. Not in his mess, but through his mess. True love is a development and enveloped in a bond of truth, commitment, and trust. Notice that it is truth and trust that keeps commitment as the center focus of the relationship. A man may find it hard to find a wife if he doesn't have a committed relationship with God—one built on truth and trust. First of all, the man should be true to himself and others, which will be pleasing to God. Second, he has to trust God in all things because he's relying on his true relationship with Him. This will bring in the needed commitment to keep the truth and trust going and growing. In order for us to trust in God, we have to first believe that He is God.

The same goes for a man and a woman. We have to trust and believe in the power of love and the relationship if we believe the relationship is worth the commitment. If a man is going to disregard a woman, then all he's saying is that he's not ready for the commitment. If he's not ready, then it's okay for her to keep on leaving and preparing.

Preparing for what, you might ask?

Well, preparing for the day that his eyes are opened; and if she is still around, he will see her. If not, then he will be prepared to see what he missed out on. This is not the end of the world for her or him. He will have the opportunity to see another woman, and the good thing for him and her is that he should be wide-awake.

HER WORTH

Finally getting to that place of understanding her worth, the question is and could be: when is he going to see her for what she is really worth? The real question is when is she going to see her self-worth? No one is going to truly value her for her if she doesn't value herself. It's all fine and well to esteem others. However, in the midst of esteeming others, she can't forget her self-esteeming obligation.

One of the main reasons that it's difficult for a woman to leave a situation that she wasn't made to be in is the fact that she can only see herself through his eyes. However, if his eyes don't reflect the woman that she is, then it's a great possibility that his eyes are not for her alone.

It's my belief that a man should see his woman the way that she is and was created to be for him. Even though he may not always get everything he wants, she'll be that one thing he needs. He should feel her love she has for him and not take advantage of her vulnerability.

The one thing that surprises many women is that men may think that she is dumb. And this statement has been made in my presence before, that women are dumb and men are stupid. After pondering the thought I came to the conclusion that women are not stupid, and men are only dumb for thinking that she is.

I always wondered if many people think God is dumb because He doesn't judge us the way we truly deserve to be judged. He's so faithful in who He is towards us that He doesn't think like we think, or act in ways that we act. Just because He isn't on us the moment we show signs of infidelity or mistrust doesn't mean He's oblivious to what's going on. He is just, loving, pure, and faithful.

Sounds just like a woman to me.

A woman isn't stupid just because she doesn't call a man out on everything that she sees as a sign or red flag. He may feel like he's getting by with things or getting away with things, but she can see a lot of things. Why does she not call him out on everything, you may ask? It's because she is fashioned to give man a chance to see what he has been presented, a gift.

As a woman, my advice to help a man to truly understand is this: Never underestimate the power of a woman. Never get to a place where you think she doesn't know what you are really all about. She saw you before you saw her. She knows when you are sleeping even when you appear to be awake. She knows when you've been bad or good just by the roads you choose to take. In essence, what I'm saying is that many women have a third eye, a sixth sense; however, she sometimes chooses to ignore it. The why may be different for different women, but the bottom line is the same. It's because she's a nurturer by nature and created to be naughty.

Yes, men, women are not much different from the man. She can be just as corrupt with nature as a man if she so desires. She has the ability to do and operate just as a man does, but what cost to her character is she willing to pay? If she decides that she's going to be like a man, she's considered a whore or a slut. When a man isn't reflecting the image of God, he's considered to be a dog, an animal. One derogatory and the other acting like something that is socially unacceptable. The connection of the two is that both of them depreciate in value when they act in this manner. It's a depreciative value in society that makes both men and women separate from God.

This is why it's hard for a man to find a wife and for a woman to believe the man that says she's "the one." The one what? Is she the one that he's going to try to manipulate like all the others he's deceived in the past? Or the one that he's going to love, respect, and cherish because his eyes have been opened?

If a man is going to eventually find a wife, he's going to have to commit to the ways of a man that's walking around with his eyes opened. Eventually, this man's going to have to finally come to his senses and realize that God won't continue to give His gifts to dogs.

GIVING HER BACK TO GOD WILL SILENCE HER WOES
What will cause her to ponder her existence lies in the thoughts of man concerning her and her well-being. She believes that being well is where she's supposed to be at all times: well organized, well understood, and well taken care of.

Sometimes this can seem like a foreign matter to a man because he may not understand how well she may or may not be doing. The woman may not always expose her woes because she has discovered that this moan may frighten a man; however, it is important for her to be transparent.

When the man finds her, he has to understand that the deepest cries can only be silenced when he has a relationship with God and his wife. Trying to understand her alone is complicated and can lead to many misunderstandings. She was designed to carry things, but he was formed to handle that which she was assigned to carry. In other words, her assignment is linked to his handle and together they can overcome many obstacles if he remains open to handling her openness.

Her heart matters…

HER HEART TRULY MATTERS

The heart of a woman does matter. Regardless of how a man may refuse to see her heart, it does matter and we shall find out why. The first thing that a woman needs to realize is that her heart matters to God. Man looks at the outward appearance, but God looks at the heart. What the woman needs to be careful of is whom she chooses to give her heart to.

As a woman I have learned firsthand that a man will take what you decide to give. In other words, if you choose to give him your heart before he's ready to receive it, trust me, he will take it. The woman was presented to the man as a fashioned individual. As the man took a look at her, it is clear that he wasn't able to see her heart because of his reaction to what he was able to look upon. The woman standing in the presence of the man is a clear indication that her heart mattered to God. He was so delicate in his design of the woman that He chose to fashion her from the rib and not the man's heart.

The heart is where the emotions are stored, even in the heart of the man. Their beings have opposite everything; but the hearts are their commonality. In my opinion, the woman was not fashioned from the man's heart because she and he have different emotions. She was fashioned from his rib, which is used to support his structure. Her position in his heart is not to fancy his emotions, but to support his creation or his foundation. God created Eve to support His creation. The rib does that for the natural body as the spirit does that for the spiritual being.

Woman, giving your heart to a man is the wrong thing to do. You should focus on leaving your heart in God's hand, the One that created you in his likeness. He is the only One that knows just how much your heart matters.

This isn't to say that a woman shouldn't love the man with her heart, but she should consider not loving him with her emotions. The woman's heart truly matters because she has to bear what really matters, and that's her assignment. The man by nature will take what he's given, even before he knows how to handle it. When a woman gives her heart to a man, especially the wrong man, she's off the rib. In other words, she's not strong enough to support that which she was created to support. Thinking about the hurt and the pain that another human being can cause the heart can sometimes be unbearable, meaning intolerable, which is a sign that she's not in fellowship with her assignment. A woman that's not able to tolerate her assignment before she is proposed to may simply mean that he's not the man for her.

This may be a hard pill to swallow, but a man that knows the value of his heart will always consider the value of hers. If all he thinks about is himself, then he's not ready for her. Her heart is delicate and he needs to not try to encounter it if he's not willing to make his heart one with hers. This simply means that when a man finds a wife, he's ready, prepared, and eager to make that heart commitment—that emotional promise to love her as Christ loved the Church. She'll become his sweetheart, his dear, his honey, and his one.

Secondly, the way to arrive at the point of knowing your heart matters as a woman is to maintain a posture or position in God that allows you to guard your heart. A woman is to look out for her heart and not entrust it to a man to do so. This isn't to say that she shouldn't entrust her emotions to her husband, but this isn't where it all starts. Looking out for your heart allows you to know that your husband has finally found you as his wife. A woman should always consider herself before giving of herself for another to consider what he thinks should be considered of her. Knowing how much the woman's heart matters is a matter of fact. It does matter and it should matter just as much to her as it matters to the One that created it.

If the man is considering taking the responsibility of caring for a woman's heart, then he has a huge task. However, he can't be totally responsible for her heart—he's only accountable for how he chooses to treat her. She has the responsibility to herself to ensure that she's not giving the man a task that she is to *share* with him. She has to know that her heart matters to *her*, if to no one else.

The last thing that a woman should know about her heart is that when she knows how much it matters, she'll be more careful who she opens it up to. She won't be so willing to open up her emotions to a man that isn't capable of handling the delicacy of who she is. She is extremely beautiful and brilliantly complete within herself. She may struggle with knowing who she is and just how much her heart matters when she feels incomplete. When a man finds a wife, he needs to know that he has found a complete human being. When a man finds a wife, he knows her heart matters because he sees how she cares for herself and how she's not willing to give it to anyone that doesn't appreciate it. When a man finds a wife, he increases the value of her heart. Her heart now matters to him.

THAT PART OF THE BODY

When a man finds a wife, he discovers the part of the body of Christ that is considered an intricate part of the man's responsibility to love and care for. In other words, this is a sometimes complicated yet sophisticated part of the body that man was commanded to love as Christ loves the Church—so much that He gave His life for it in such a physical and spiritual way.

The sacrifice of giving is the form in which Christ gave of Himself for the body of Christ, or the Church. In today's society the true believer of love knows what it means to sacrifice and give of oneself. Trying to understand why the sacrifice has to be made lies in the details of Christ's gift of giving for us all. Christ dying for our sins was and is the true symbol of sacrificing and giving. The most interesting part of the way a man would give of himself to save the lost is mind blowing; especially when he is deity or divine. The man that God created in the beginning was and is yet a part of the divinity, given the fact that he was created in God's imagine and in His likeness.

When a Man Finds a Wife, He Discovers the Inside of God

The man of God knowing who he is in a concrete manner can help him to love and care for the things the Creator has given to him. The man is given an assignment to love the wife or the woman that he's to connect his life to. He's to love her as the broad essence of his existence he was created for.

He was created as an extension of who? Our Father. The assignment to subdue and dominate the earth is great in that it's not only impressive, but big. How can he do all of this in his human form? The answer is with the connection to the Creator. The assignment wasn't given without the man being equipped to handle the task. The man was provided everything he needed on the inside of him to complete the task of naming everything that he was given, even the woman. Now that she's brought out of him and placed in front of him, he can see and express what he is feeling. She's here to help him with the expressions that he tries so often to suppress. This is only when he's connected to the woman that he has named as his, his wife.

How does the connection come into existence and when should he make this official? When he realizes that she understands him and he gets her. In other words, she can be the one that he makes his wife and he can see himself developing in her. He gets to help her grow and become who she was created to be for him through development.

This is why she was created to be for him. Together they were ordered to be fruitful and multiply. Together they can be productive and successful while increasing and growing.

If this order isn't being fulfilled in the relationship, then it may be the wrong connection. Many relationships are not ordained or intended to be, because this order isn't being filled. The way to make sure that a prescription is effective is when it's been filled and used. When something is prescribed, it's given to make the patient better. The only way that the patient can get better is if he or she actually follows the physician's orders. The order is the command or instructions.

The way to establish and ensure that the man has found his wife is in the process of his understanding the Doctors' orders. In this case, he is to follow the Creator's orders for his life. Listening to God and understanding what his assignment and talents are helps him to get just what he needs to complete his assignment. The woman for him can help him with his assignment as he gets to help her with hers. The relationship is not productive if they're not able to push each other to success and increase in growth. He's concerned about her ability to grow with him and she's concerned about his not being stunted or stuck in his growing process. Together they are after the success they were commanded to obtain together. It's easy to do things separately, but the multiplication comes when the two come together as one. They are two times greater when the one is multiplied by the two. **The two are one in the eyes of the multiplier.**

It's simple when they both get it together. He has to be open and ready to receive her, and she has to be in place when he is ready. This doesn't mean a woman has to wait on a man to get himself together; she has to know whether or not she's his presentation. She'll know if she's his production because he'll make the necessary eye adjustments for her. In other words, he'll make the changes to include her in his already created and existing life. The adjustment has to be made when he sees what God has given to him. He's not to disregard her heart, because she is ready to protect his. The matters and substance of her heart should matter to him because she's a material that comes from him. He should be concerned with her growth and development because she is there to help him complete the charge and responsibilities that he's been given. Since she's now physically out of him, she can help him to understand what he might be feeling. He has to allow her the opportunity to do what she was present and presented to do.

ABOUT THE AUTHOR

☙

Sherrie Norwood is a prolific author, licensed and ordained pastor, and compelling speaker currently residing in Orlando, Florida. She has a vast background in non-profit organizations that includes multiple certifications and trainings. Sherrie has a passion for helping individuals and families find purpose as they create and maintain stable foundations. She holds a Bachelor of Science degree in Human Service Management and a Master of Science degree in Psychology from the University of Phoenix. She is a business writing expert and consultant. Sherrie's call of duty also includes having served proudly in the United States Army, but by far her greatest accomplishment is being the proud mother of her three adult children: Shanee, Perscell (PJ), and Shaneice; and her glam-daughter, Michae'la!

This is just the start of many…